BALLAD OF A TEENAGE QUEEN

Words and Music by
JACK CLEMENT

1. There's a sto - ry in our town of the pret - ti - est
2. She was tops in all, they said. It nev - er once __ went
3. He would mar - ry her next spring. Saved his mon - ey,
4., 5. *(See additional lyrics)*

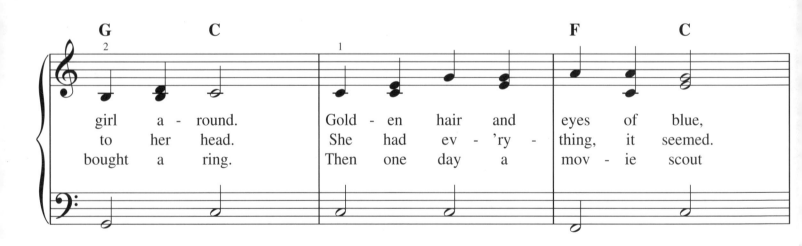

girl a - round.   Gold - en hair and   eyes of blue,
to her head.   She had ev - 'ry -   thing, it seemed.
bought a ring.   Then one day a   mov - ie scout

how those eyes could flash at you.
Not a care, this teen - age queen.
came to town to take her out.

(How those eyes could
(Not a care, this
(Came to town to

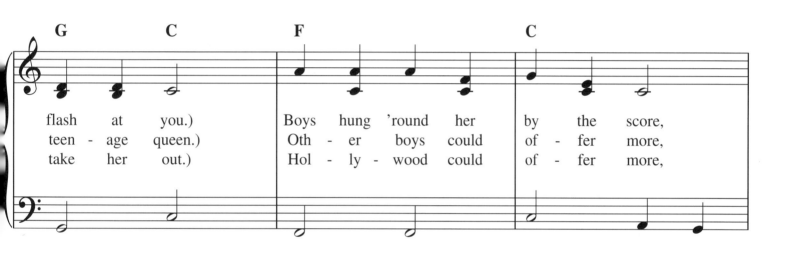

flash at you.) Boys hung 'round her by the score,
teen - age queen.) Oth - er boys could of - fer more,
take her out.) Hol - ly - wood could of - fer more,

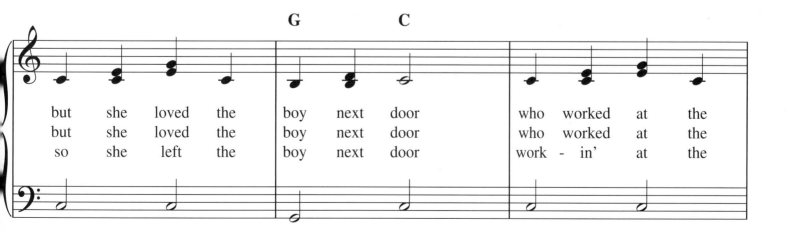

but she loved the boy next door who worked at the
but she loved the boy next door who worked at the
so she left the boy next door work - in' at the

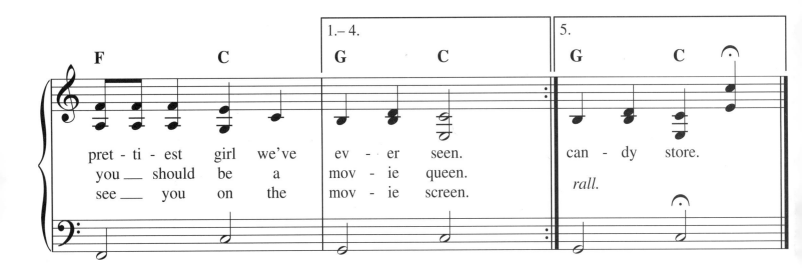

Additional Lyrics

4. Very soon she was a star, pretty house and shiny cars,
   Swimming pool and a fence around, but she missed her old home town.
   (But she missed her old home town.)
   All the world was at her door,
   All except the boy next door who worked at the candy store.
   Dream on, dream on, teenage queen, saddest girl we've ever seen.

5. Then one day the teenage star sold her house and all her cars.
   Gave up all her wealth and fame, left it all and caught a train.
   (Left it all and caught a train.)
   Do I have to tell you more?
   She came back to the boy next door who worked at the candy store.
   Now this story has some more. You'll hear it at the candy store.

FOLSOM PRISON BLUES

Words and Music by
JOHN R. CASH

1. I

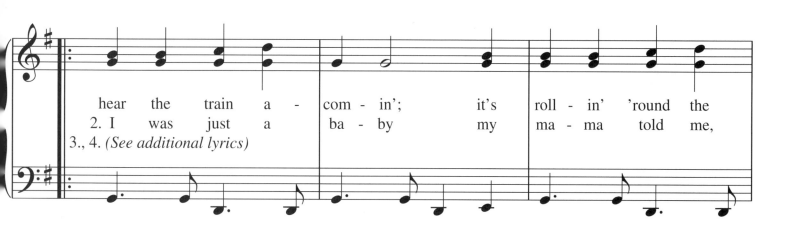

hear the train a - com - in'; it's roll - in' 'round the
2. I was just a ba - by my ma - ma told me,
3., 4. *(See additional lyrics)*

bend and I ain't seen the sun - shine since
"Son, al - ways be a good boy; since don't

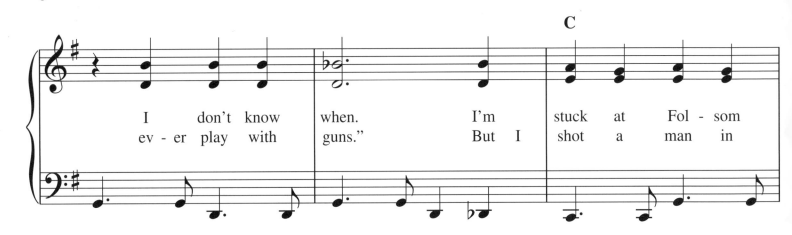

I don't know when. I'm stuck at Fol - som
ev - er play with guns." But I shot a man in

Pri - son and time keeps drag - gin'
Re - no just keeps to watch him

G

on.
die.

D7

But that train keeps roll - in'
When I hear that whis - tle blow - in'

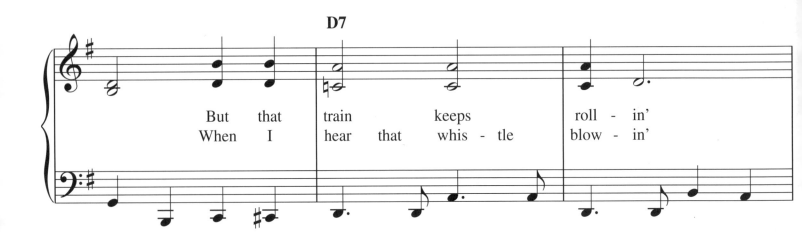

on down to San ___ An - tone. ___
I hang my head ___ and ___ cry. ___

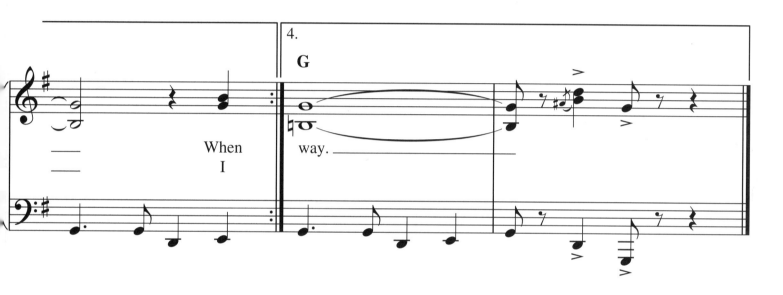

When way. ___
I

Additional Lyrics

3. I bet there's rich folks eatin' in a fancy dining car.
   They're prob'ly drinkin' coffee and smokin' big cigars.
   But I know I had it comin', I know I can't be free,
   But those people keep a-movin', and that's what tortures me.

4. Well, if they freed me from this prison, if that railroad train was mine,
   I bet I'd move on over a little farther down the line.
   Far from Folsom Prison, that's where I want to stay,
   And I'd let that lonesome whistle blow my blues away.

A BOY NAMED SUE

Words and Music by
SHEL SILVERSTEIN

Moderately bright

1. *(Spoken:)* Well, my

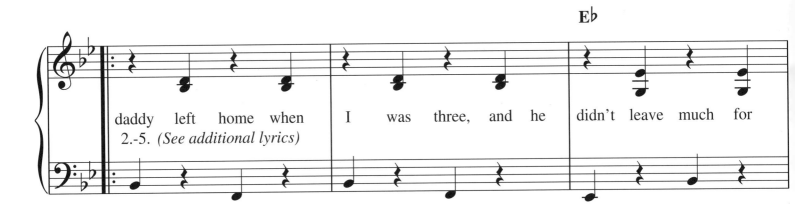

daddy left home when I was three, and he didn't leave much for
2.-5. *(See additional lyrics)*

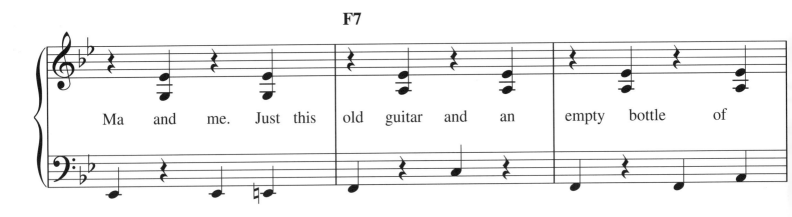

Ma and me. Just this old guitar and an empty bottle of

booze. Now, I don't blame him because he run and hid, but the

meanest thing that he | ever did was be - | fore he left, he

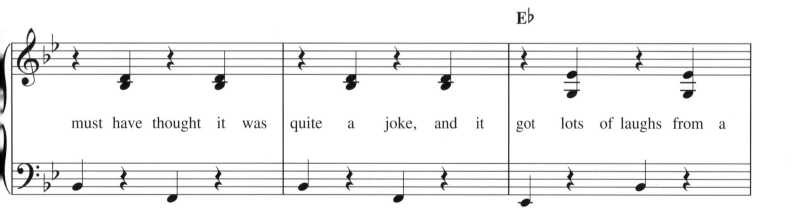

went and named me Sue. | | | Well, he

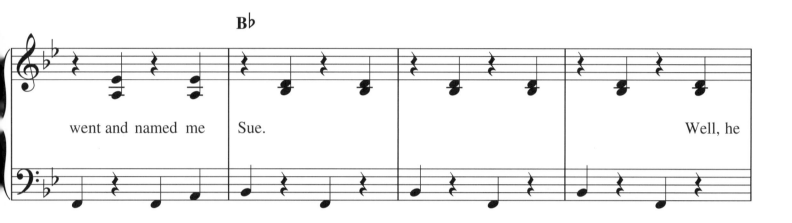

must have thought it was | quite a joke, and it | got lots of laughs from a

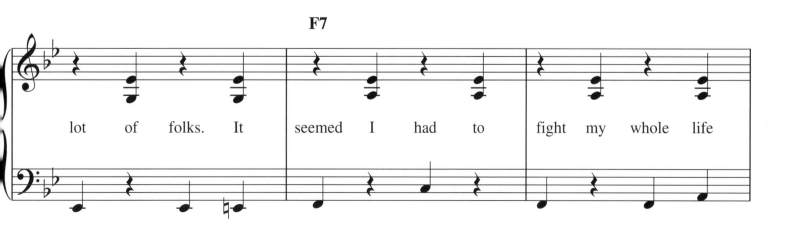

lot of folks. It | seemed I had to | fight my whole life

through.   Some gal would giggle and

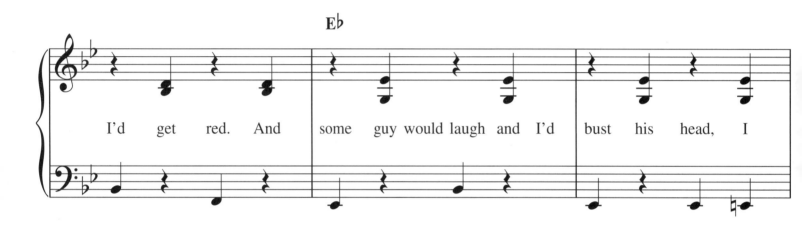

I'd get red. And some guy would laugh and I'd bust his head, I

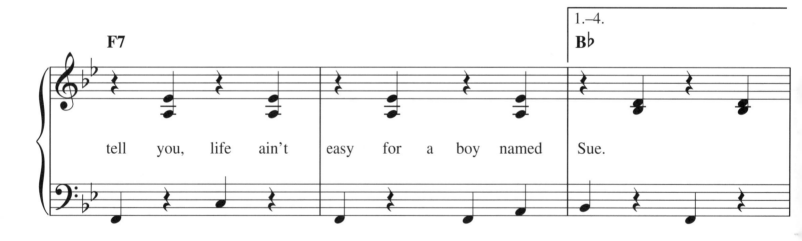

tell you, life ain't easy for a boy named Sue.

Well,   Sue.

Additional Lyrics

2. Well, I grew up quick and I grew up mean,
My fist got hard and my wits got keen.
I'd roam from town to town to hide my shame.
But I made a vow to the moon and stars
That I'd search the honky-tonks and bars
And kill that man who gave me that awful name.

Well, it was Gatlinburg in mid-July
And I had just hit town and my throat was dry,
I thought I'd stop and have myself a brew.
At an old saloon on a street of mud,
There at a table, dealing stud,
Sat the dirty, mangy dog that named me Sue.

3. Well, I knew that snake was my own sweet dad
From a worn-out picture that my mother'd had,
And I knew that scar on his cheek and his evil eye.
He was big and bent and gray and old,
And I looked at him and my blood ran cold
And I said: "My name is Sue! How do you do?
Now you're gonna die!"

Well, I hit him hard right between the eyes
And he went down, but to my surprise,
He come up with a knife and cut off a piece of my ear.
But I busted a chair right across his teeth
And we crashed through the wall and into the street
Kicking and a-gouging in the mud and the blood and the beer.

4. I tell ya, I've fought tougher men,
But I really can't remember when.
He kicked like a mule and he bit like a crocodile.
I heard him laugh and then I heard him cuss,
He went for his gun and I pulled mine first.
He stood there lookin' at me and I saw him smile.

And he said: "Son, this world is rough
And if a man's gonna make it, he's gotta be tough
And I knew I wouldn't be there to help you along.
So I give you that name and I said goodbye.
I knew you'd have to get tough or die.
And it's the name that helped to make you strong."

5. He said: "Now you just fought one hell of a fight
And I know you hate me, and you got the right
To kill me now, and I wouldn't blame you if you do.
But you ought to thank me, before I die,
For the gravel in your guts and the spit in your eye,
'Cause I'm the son-of-a-bitch that named you Sue."

I got all choked up and I threw down my gun.
And I called him my pa, and he called me his son,
And I came away with a different point of view.
And I think about him, now and then,
Every time I try and every time I win,
And if I ever have a son, I think I'm gonna name him
Bill or George! Anything but Sue!

CRY, CRY, CRY

Words and Music by
JOHN R. CASH

Moderately, in 2

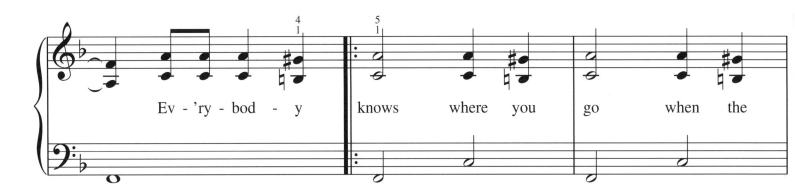

Ev - 'ry - bod - y knows where you go when the

sun goes down. I think you on - ly

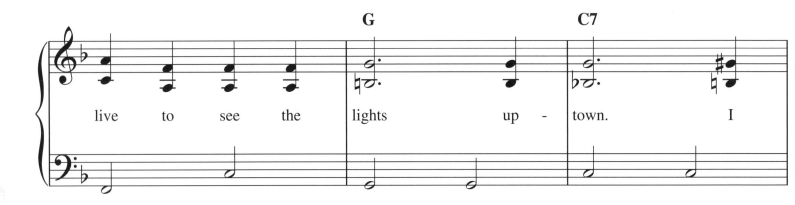

live to see the lights up - town. I

wast - ed my time when I would try, try,

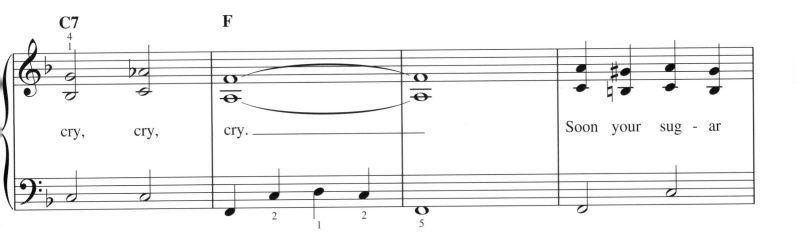

try, 'cause when the lights have lost their glow, you'll

cry, cry, cry. Soon your sug - ar

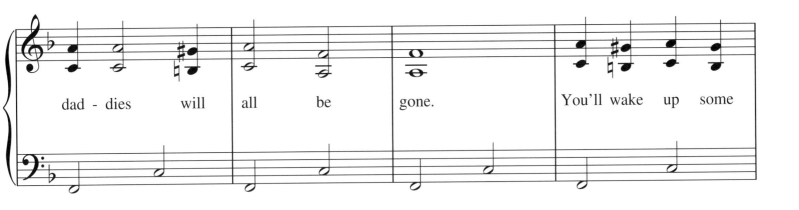

dad - dies will all be gone. You'll wake up some

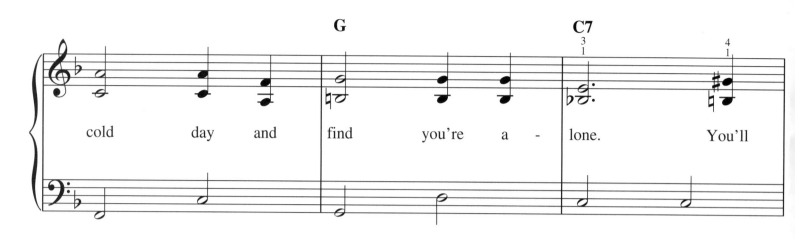

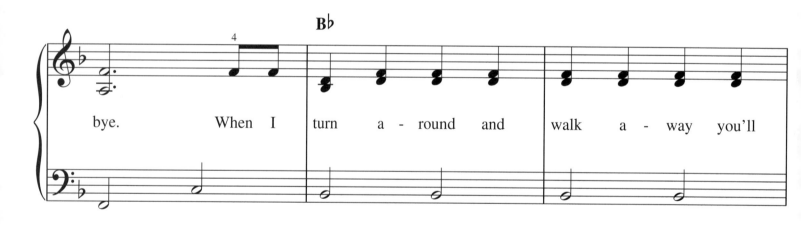

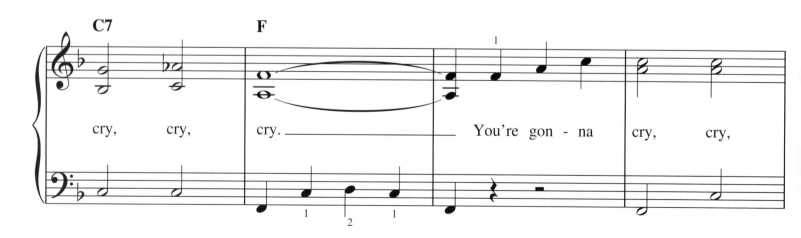

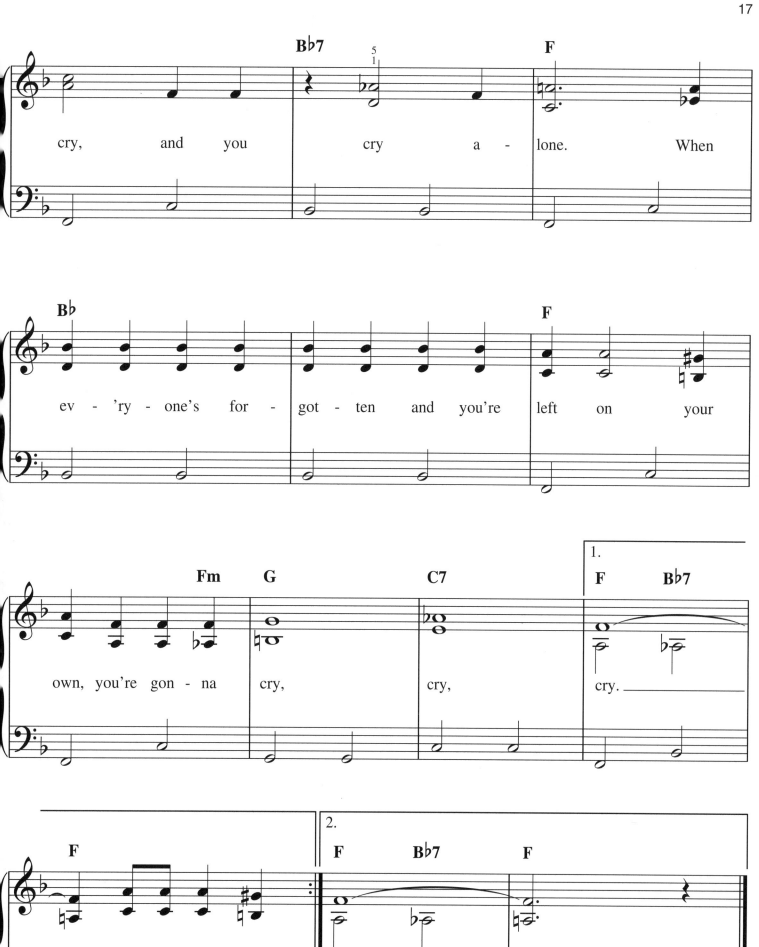

DON'T TAKE YOUR GUNS TO TOWN

Words and Music by
JOHN R. CASH

Freely
N.C.

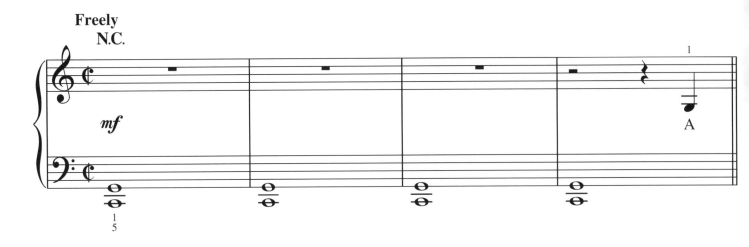

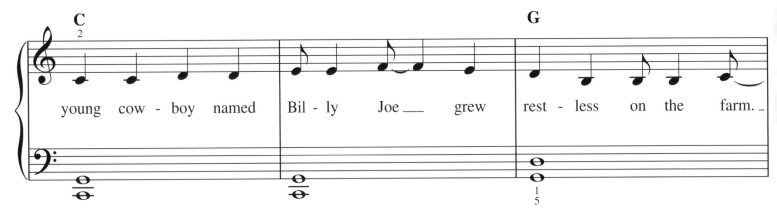

young cow - boy named   Bil - ly   Joe ___   grew   rest - less   on   the   farm. ___

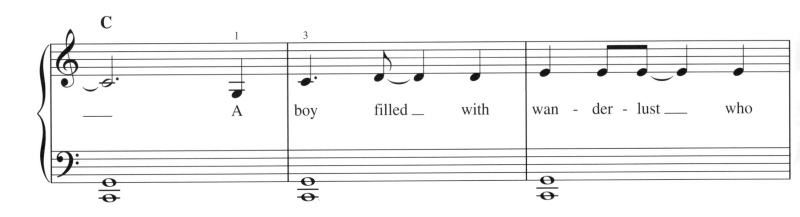

___   A   boy   filled ___ with   wan - der - lust ___   who

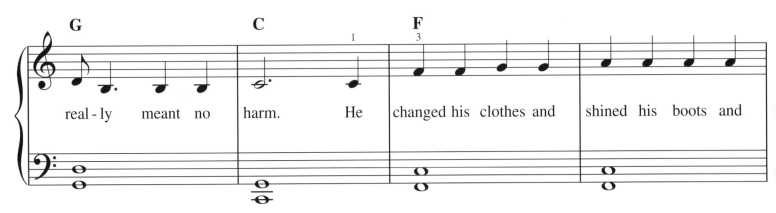

real - ly   meant   no   harm.   He   changed his clothes and   shined his boots and

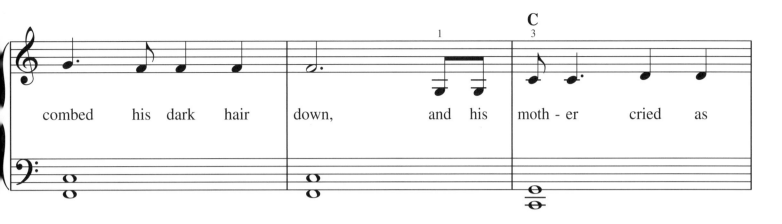

combed his dark hair down, and his moth - er cried as

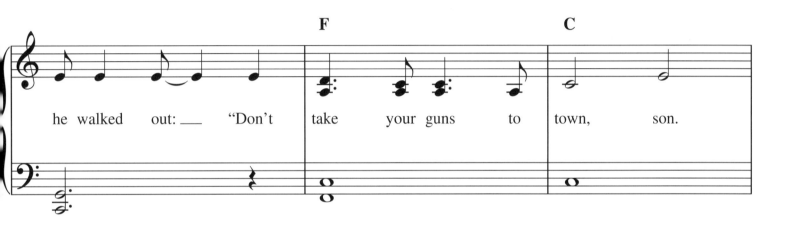

he walked out: __ "Don't take your guns to town, son.

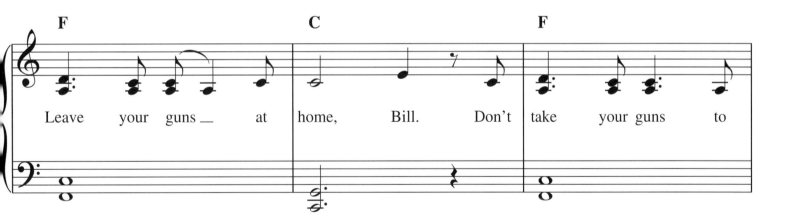

Leave your guns __ at home, Bill. Don't take your guns to

Moderately

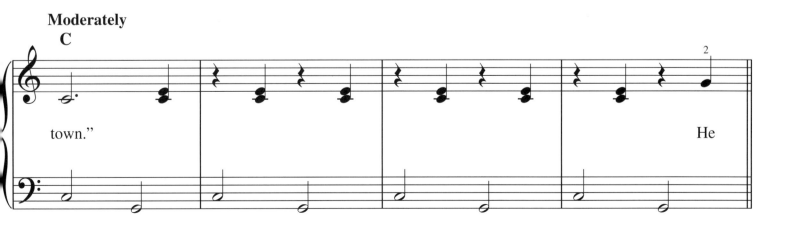

town." He

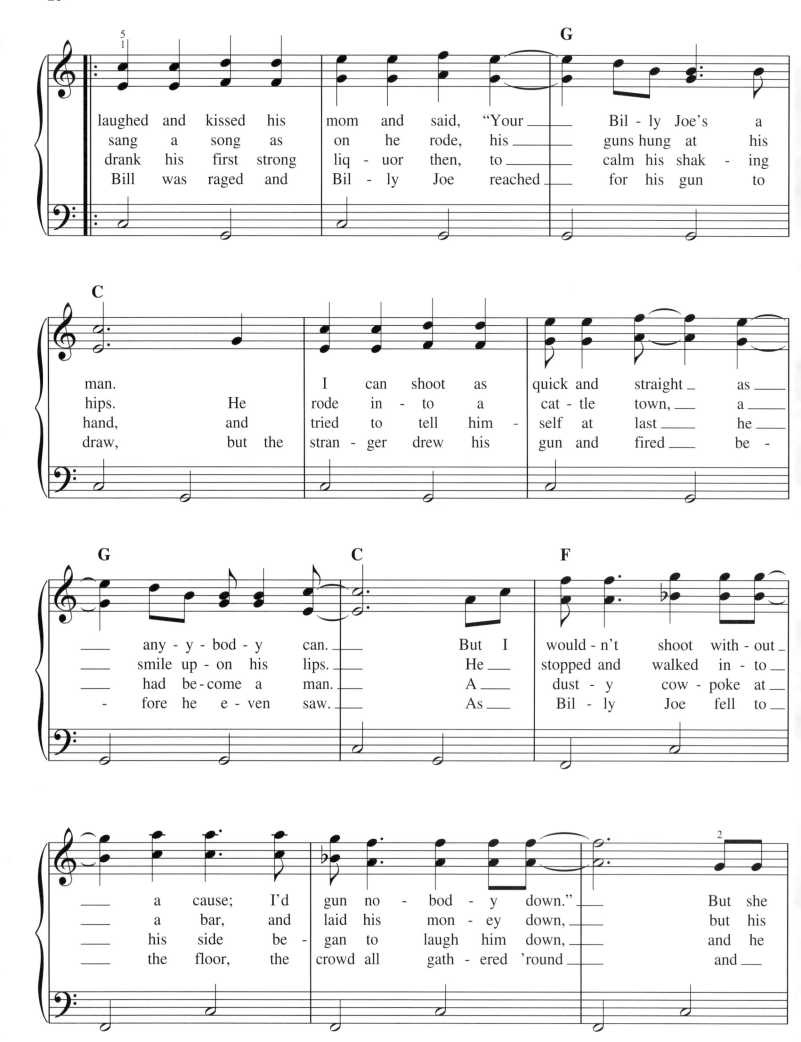

cried a - gain as he rode a - way:
moth - er's words __ ech - oed a - gain:
heard a - gain __ his moth - er's words:
won - dered at __ his fi - nal words:

"Don't take your guns to

town, Son. Leave your guns __ at home, Bill. Don't take your guns to

1.–3.
Moderately, in tempo

town."

He
He

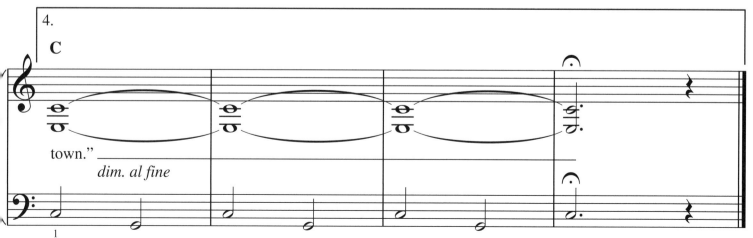

4.

town." __

dim. al fine

GET RHYTHM

Words and Music by
JOHN R. CASH

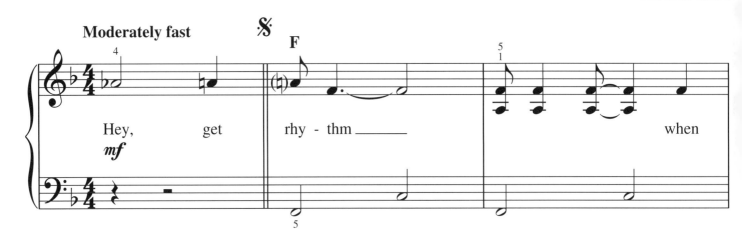

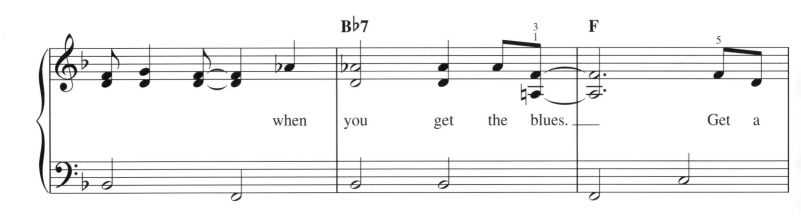

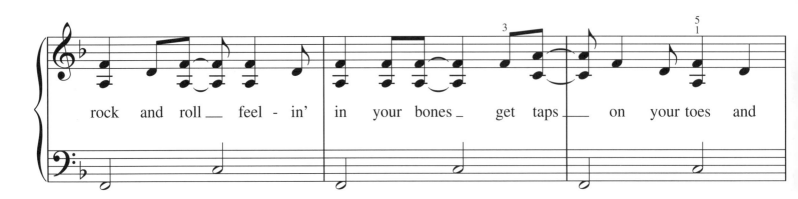

get gone, get a - rhy - thm _____ when

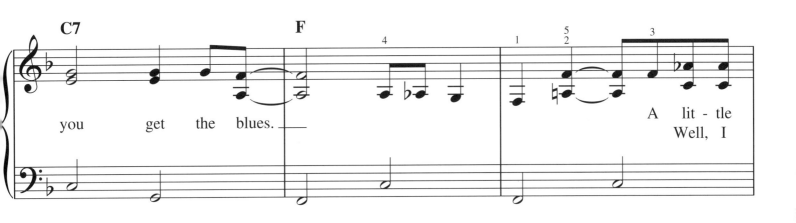

you get the blues. ____

A lit - tle
Well, I

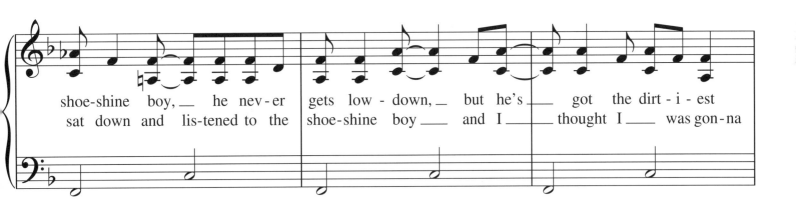

shoe-shine boy, __ he nev - er gets low - down, __ but he's ____ got the dirt - i - est
sat down and lis-tened to the shoe-shine boy ____ and I ____ thought I ____ was gon-na

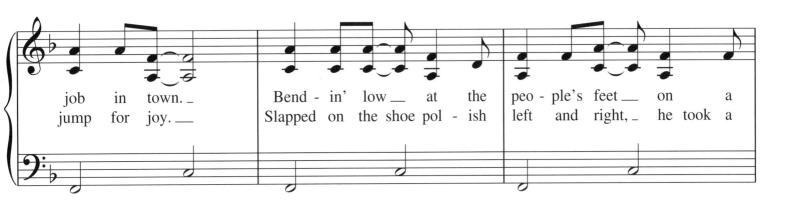

job in town. _ Bend - in' low __ at the peo - ple's feet __ on a
jump for joy. __ Slapped on the shoe pol - ish left and right, _ he took a

24

wind - y cor - ner of a dirt - y street. _ Well, I asked _ him while he
shoe - shine rag _ and _ he held it tight. _ He stopped once _ to wipe the

shined my shoes, _ how'd he keep _ from get - tin' the blues. _ He
sweat a - way. _ I said you're a might - y lit - tle boy to be work - in' that way. _ He

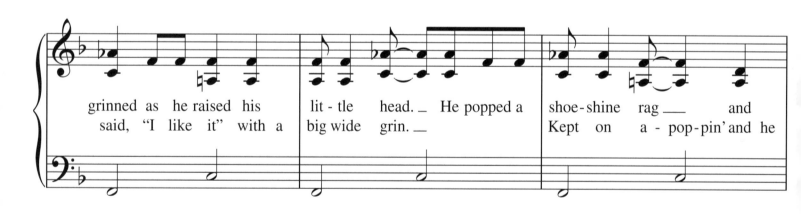

grinned as he raised his lit - tle head. _ He popped a shoe - shine rag _ and
said, "I like it" with a big wide grin. _ Kept on a - pop - pin' and he

then he said get rhy - thm _ when you get the blues. _
said a - gain

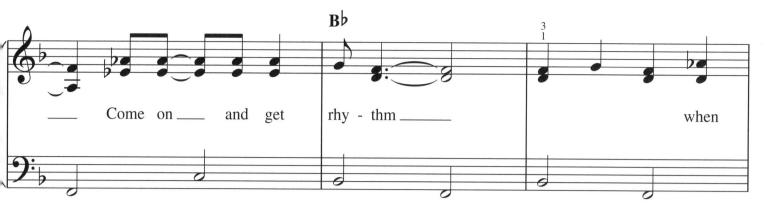

Come on ___ and get rhy - thm ___ when

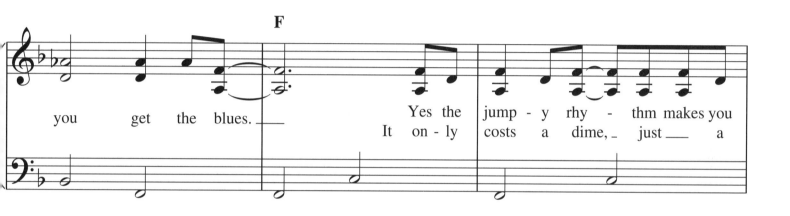

you get the blues. ___ Yes the jump - y rhy - thm makes you
It on - ly costs a dime, __ just ___ a

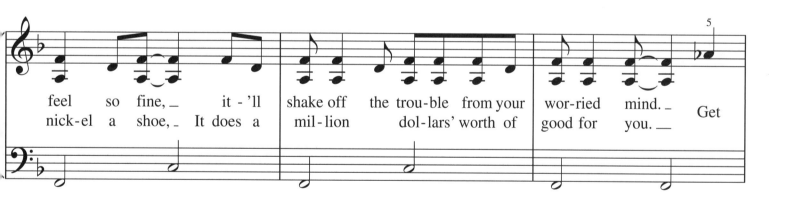

feel so fine, __ it - 'll shake off the trou-ble from your wor-ried mind. __ Get
nick-el a shoe, __ It does a mil-lion dol-lars' worth of good for you. __

To Coda

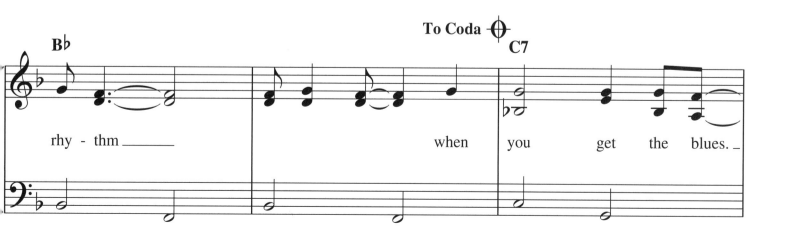

rhy - thm ___ when you get the blues. __

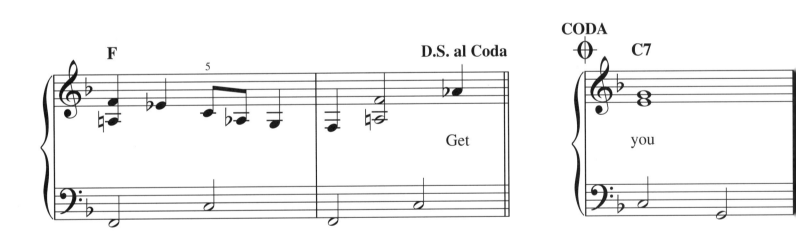

Get

you

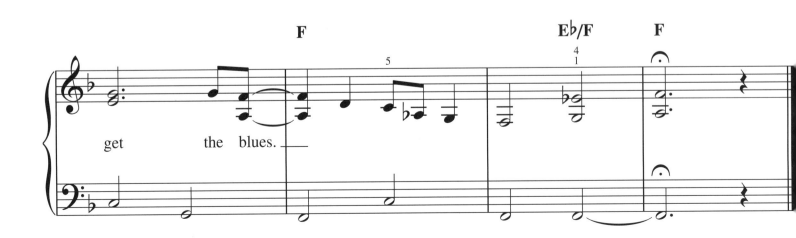

get   the   blues.

JACKSON

Words and Music by BILLY EDD WHEELER
and JERRY LEIBER

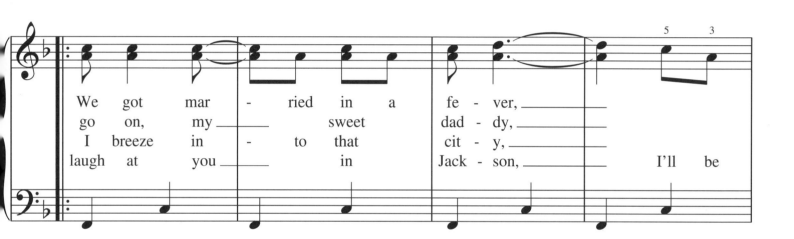

We got mar - ried in a fe - ver, _____ I'll be
go on, my _____ sweet dad - dy, _____
I breeze in - to that cit - y, _____
laugh at you _____ in Jack - son, _____

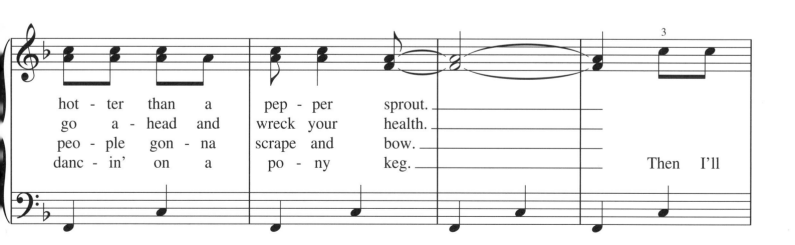

hot - ter than a pep - per sprout.
go a - head and wreck your health.
peo - ple gon - na scrape and bow. _____ Then I'll
danc - in' on a po - ny keg. _____

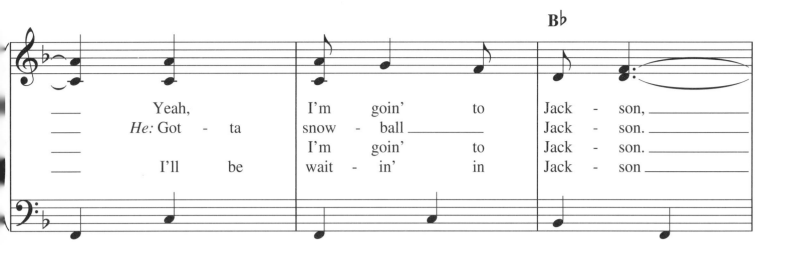

B♭

Yeah,	I'm goin' to	Jack - son,	
He: Got - ta	snow - ball _____	Jack - son.	
I'm goin' to	Jack - son.	
I'll be	wait - in' in	Jack - son	

C ... **F**

you know I'm	plea - sure	bound. _____	
She: See if I	care. _____	
"Good - bye," that's	all she	wrote. _____	
be - hind my	Ja - pan	fan. _____	

1. – 4. ... **5.**

She: Well,
He: When
She: When they

I WALK THE LINE

Words and Music by
JOHN R. CASH

Bright Country 2-beat

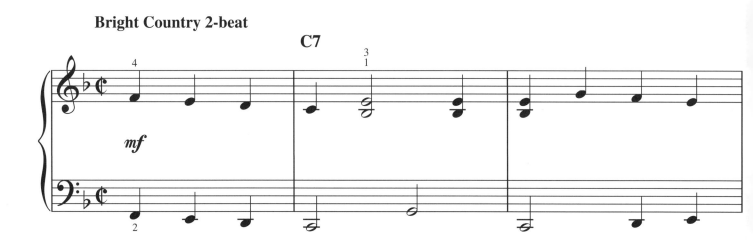

I keep a
night watch is
close watch

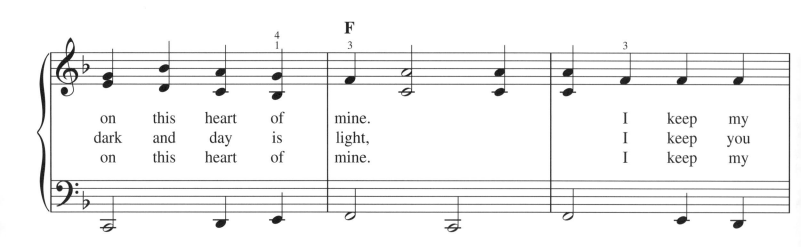

on this heart of mine. I keep my
dark and day is light, I keep you
on this heart of mine. I keep my

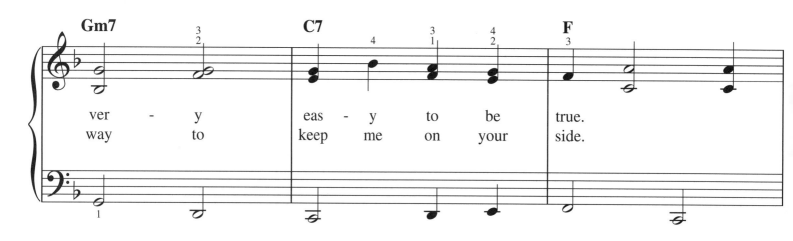

Gm7 ver - y way to

C7 eas - y to be keep me on be your

F true. side.

I find my - self a - lone
You give me cause for

Gm7 when each day is love that I can't

C7

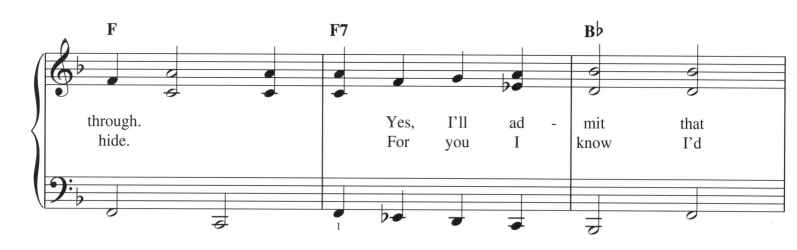

F through. hide.

F7 Yes, I'll ad - mit that For you I know that I'd

B♭

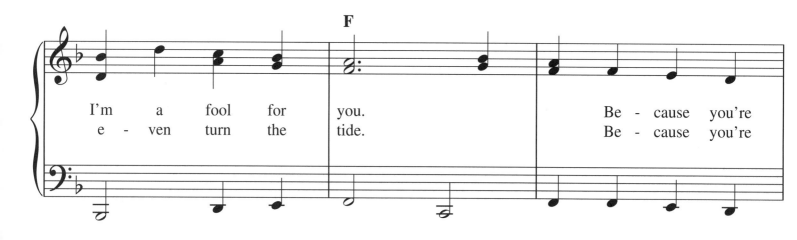

I'm a fool for e - ven turn for the

F you. tide.

Be - cause you're Be - cause you're

THE MAN IN BLACK

Words and Music by
JOHN R. CASH

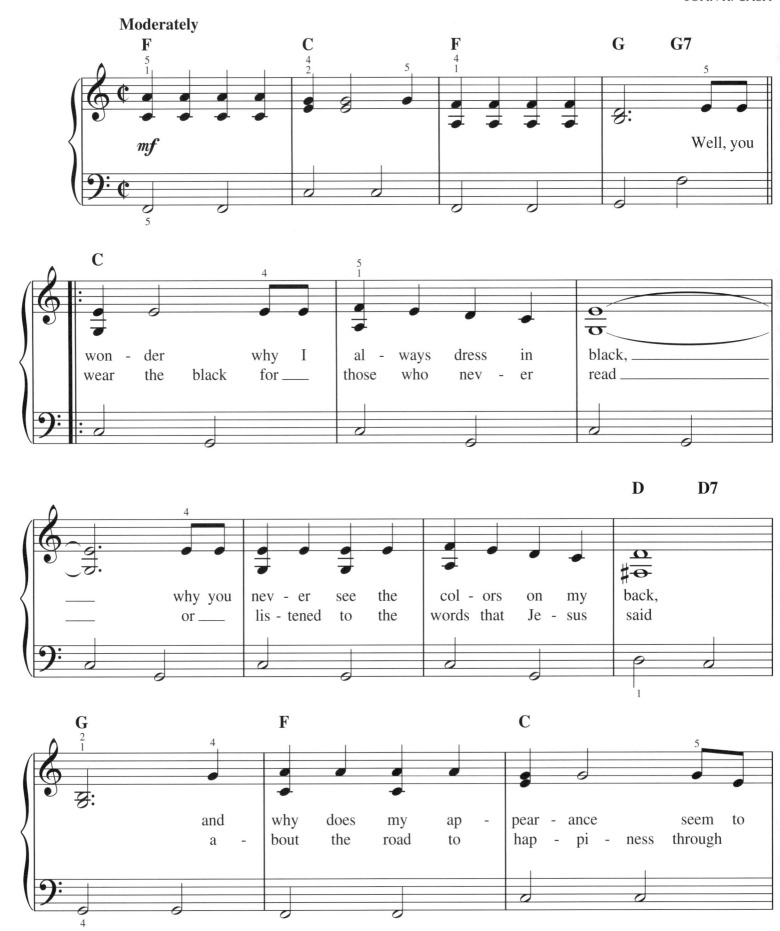

have a som - ber tone. _____ Well, there's a rea - son for the
love and char - i - ty. _____ Why, you'd think He's talk - ing

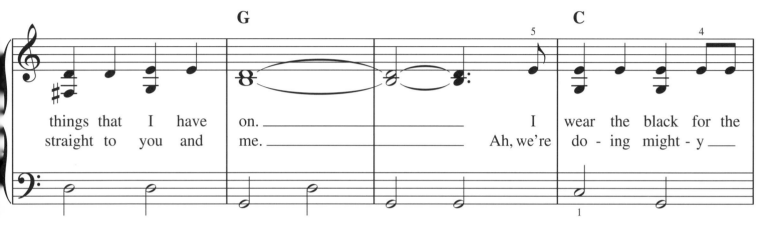

things that I have on. _____ I wear the black for the
straight to you and me. _____ Ah, we're do - ing might - y ___

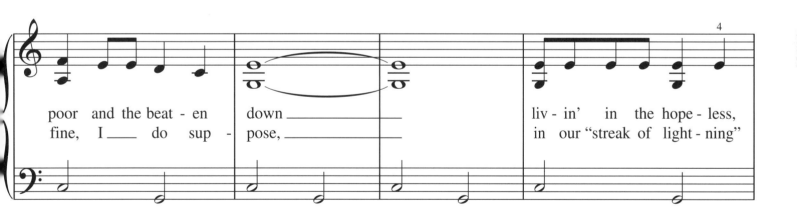

poor and the beat - en down _____ liv - in' in the hope - less,
fine, I ___ do sup - pose, _____ in our "streak of light - ning"

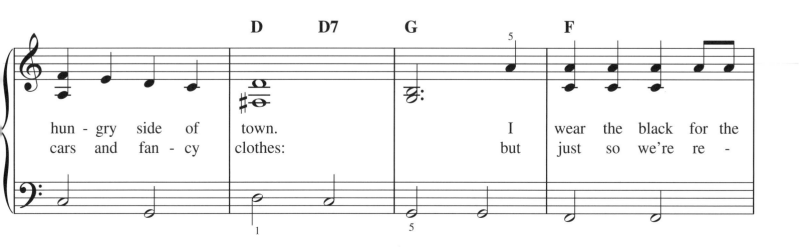

hun - gry side of town. I wear the black for the
cars and fan - cy clothes: but just so we're re -

36

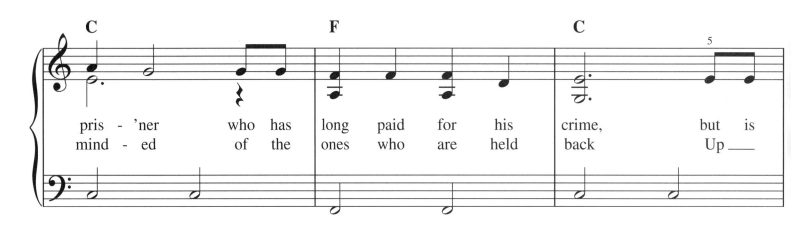

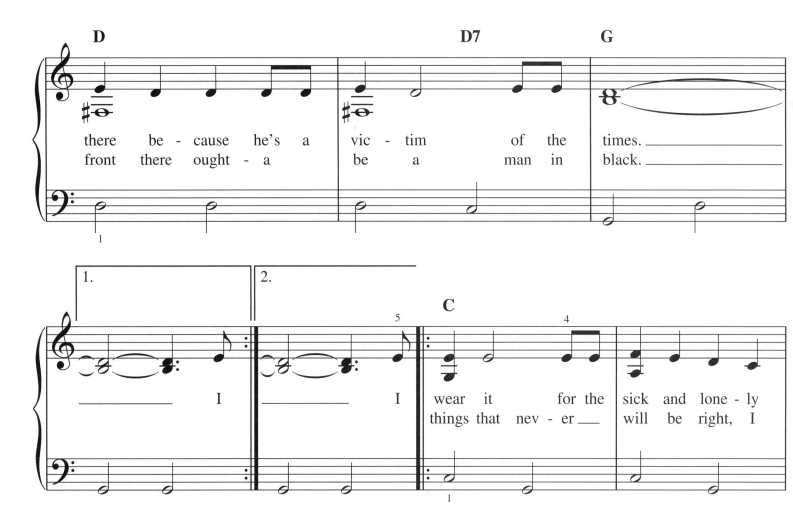

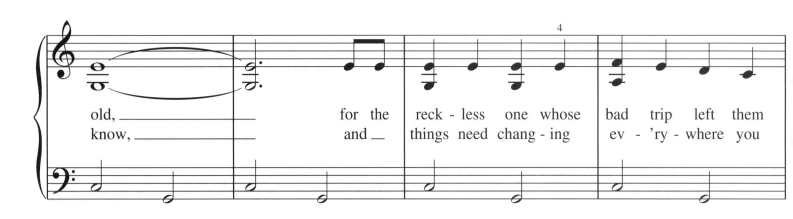

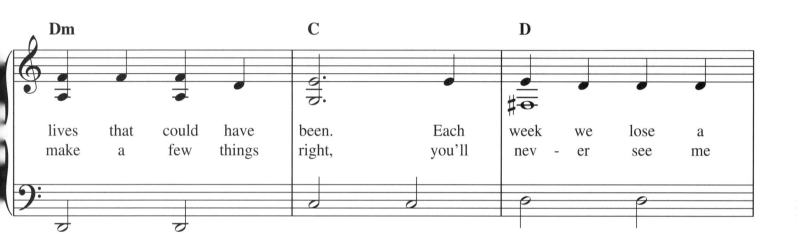

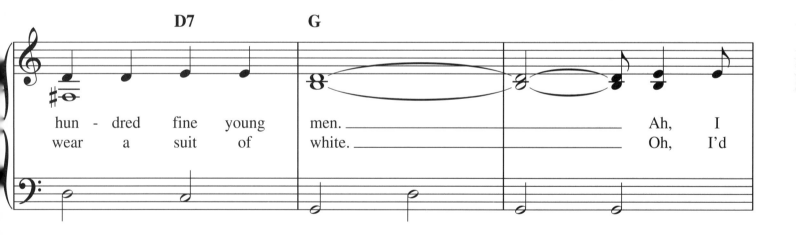

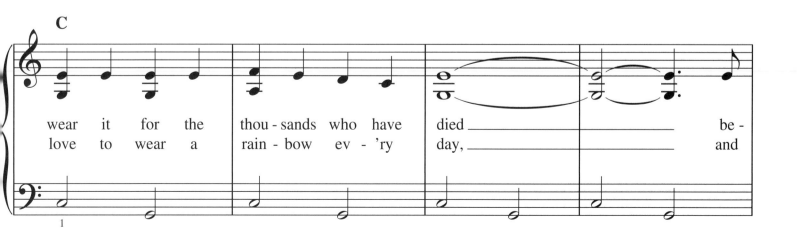

ONE PIECE AT A TIME

Words and Music by
WAYNE KEMP

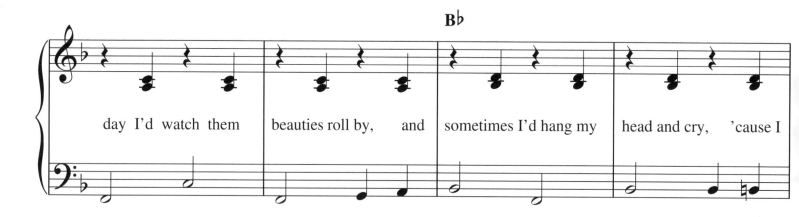

day I'd watch them beauties roll by, and sometimes I'd hang my head and cry, 'cause I

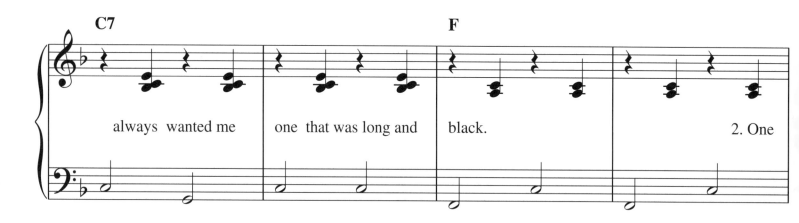

always wanted me one that was long and black. 2. One

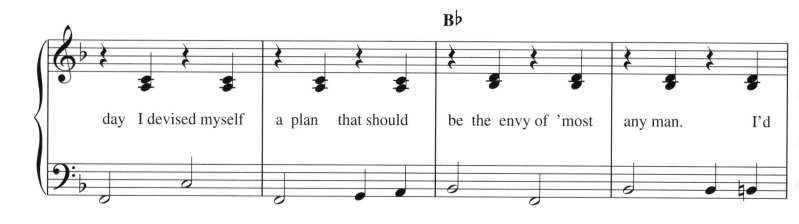

day I devised myself a plan that should be the envy of 'most any man. I'd

sneak it outta there in a lunch box in my hand. Now,

gettin' caught meant | gettin' fired, but I | figured I'd have it all by

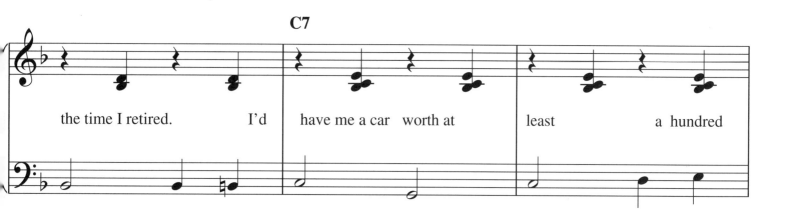

the time I retired. I'd | have me a car worth at | least a hundred

Chorus

grand. | *(Sung:)* I'd get it | one piece at a

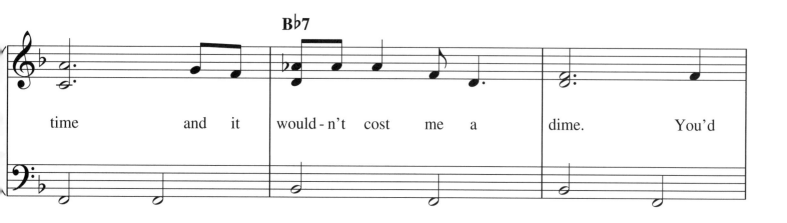

time and it | would-n't cost me a | dime. You'd

know it's me when I come through your town.

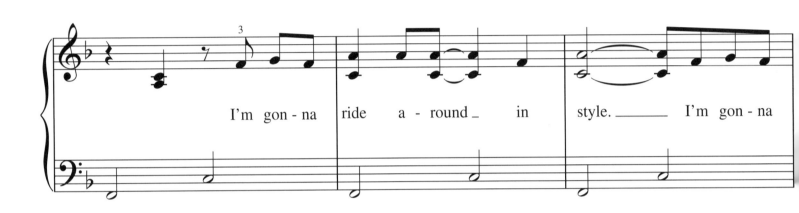

I'm gon - na ride a - round _ in style. ___ I'm gon - na

drive ev - 'ry - bod - y wild, 'cause I'll have the on - ly

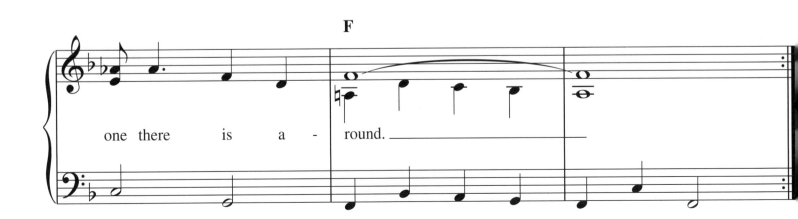

one there is a - round. ___

RECITATION

3. So, the very next day when I punched in with my big lunch box
   And with help from my friends, I left that day with a lunch box full of gears.
   I've never considered myself a thief, but GM wouldn't miss just one little piece,
   Especially if I strung it out over several years.

4. The first day, I got me a fuel pump, and the next day I got me an engine and a trunk.
   Then I got me a transmission and all the chrome.
   The little things I could get in the big lunch box,
   Like nuts and bolts and all four shocks,
   But the big stuff we snuck out in my buddy's mobile home.

5. Now, up to now, my plan went all right, 'til we tried to put it all together one night,
   And that's when we noticed that something was definitely wrong.
   The transmission was a '53, and the motor turned out to be a '73,
   And when we tried to put in the bolts, all the holes were gone.
   So, we drilled it out so that it would fit, and with a little bit of help from an adapter kit,
   We had the engine running just like a song.

6. Now the headlights, they was another sight,
   We had two on the left, and one on the right,
   But when we pulled out the switch, all three of 'em come on.
   The back end looked kinda funny, too,
   But we put it together, and when we got through,
   Well, that's when we noticed that we only had one tail fin.
   About that time, my wife walked out, and I could see in her eyes that she had her doubts,
   But she opened the door and said, "Honey, take me for a spin."

7. So, we drove uptown just to get the tags, and I headed her right on down the main drag.
   I could hear everybody laughin' for blocks around.
   But, up there at the court house, they didn't laugh,
   'Cause to type it up, it took the whole staff,
   And when they got through, the title weighed sixty pounds.

2nd Chorus: I got it one piece at a time, and it didn't cost me a dime.
   You'll know it's me when I come through your town.
   I'm gonna ride around in style. I'm gonna drive everybody wild,
   'Cause I'll have the only one there is around.

(Ad lib.): Yeah, Red Rider, this is the Cottonmouth in the Psychobilly Cadillac, com' on?
   This is the Cottonmouth, a negatory on the cost of this mo-chine, there, Red Rider.
   You might say I went right up to the factory and picked it up. It's cheaper that way.
   What model is it?... Well, it's a 49, 50, 51, 52, 53, 54, 55, 56, 57, 58, 59 automobile...
   It's a 60, 61, 62, 63, 64, 65, 66, 67, 68, 69 automobile...

RING OF FIRE

Words and Music by MERLE KILGORE
and JUNE CARTER

Moderately bright

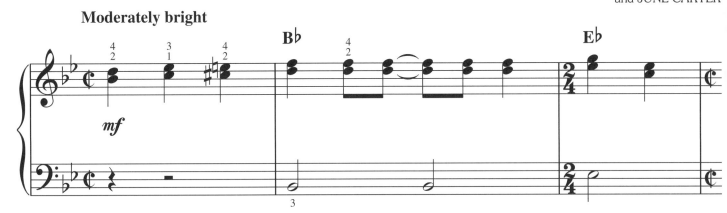

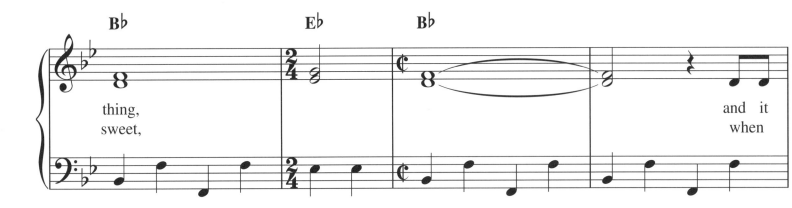

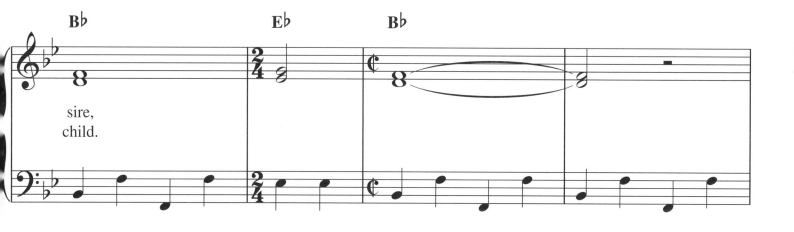

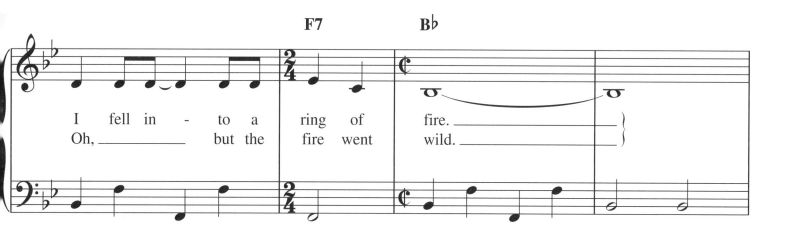

46

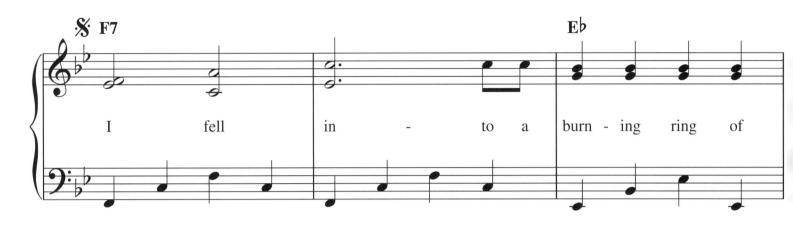

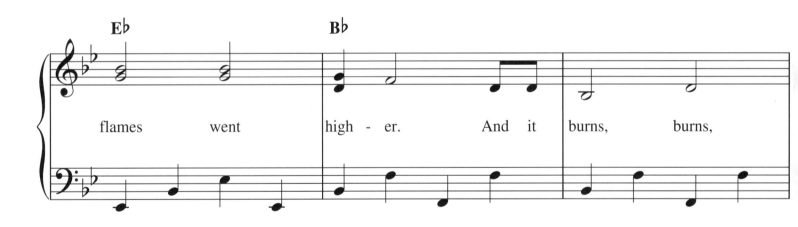

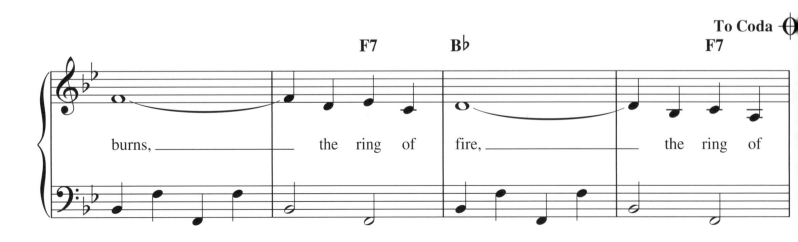

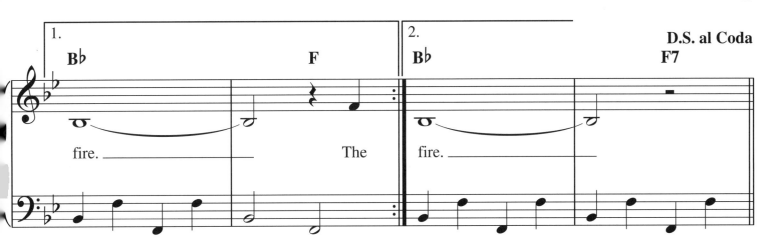

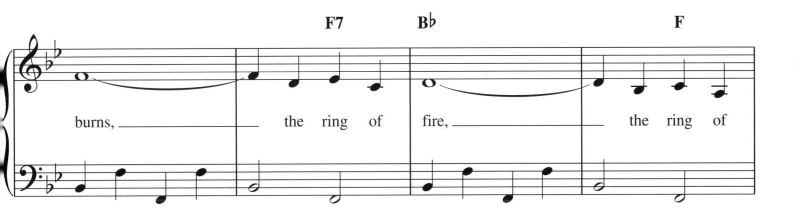

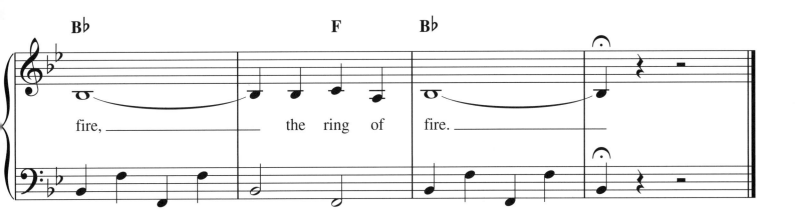

TENNESSEE FLAT TOP BOX

Words and Music by
JOHNNY CASH

Bright Country 2-beat

In a   lit - tle   cab - a - ret, __
Well, he   could-n't   ride   or wran -
Then __   one day   he   was gone __

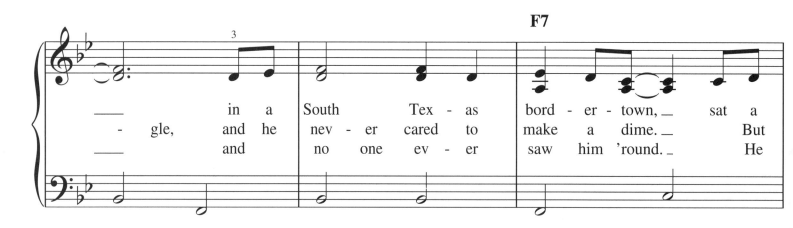

__ gle,   in a   South   Tex - as   bord - er - town, __   sat a
_ gle,   and he   nev - er   cared to   make   a   dime. __   But
__   and   no   one   ev - er   saw him 'round. __   He

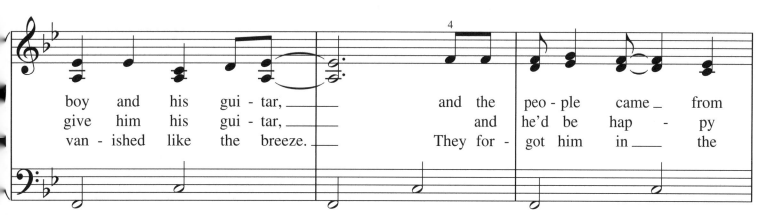

boy and his gui - tar, _____ and the peo - ple came _ from
give him his gui - tar, _____ and he'd be hap - py
van - ished like the breeze. _____ They for - got him in ___ the

all a - round. _ And all the girls
all the time. _ And all the girls
lit - tle town. _ But all the girls

from there to Aus - tin were
from nine to nine - ty were
still dreamed a - bout him and

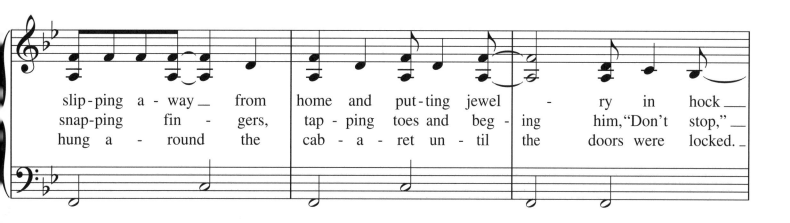

slip - ping a - way _ from home and put - ting jewel - ry in hock ___
snap - ping fin - gers, tap - ping toes and beg - ing him, "Don't stop," __
hung a - round the cab - a - ret un - til the doors were locked. _

50

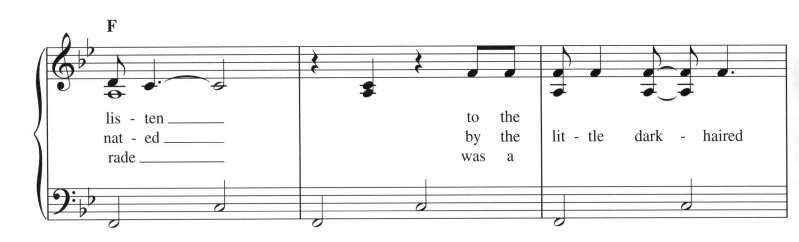

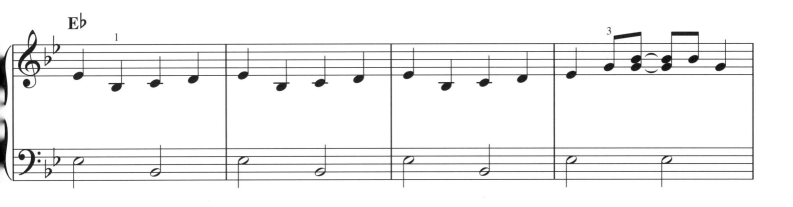

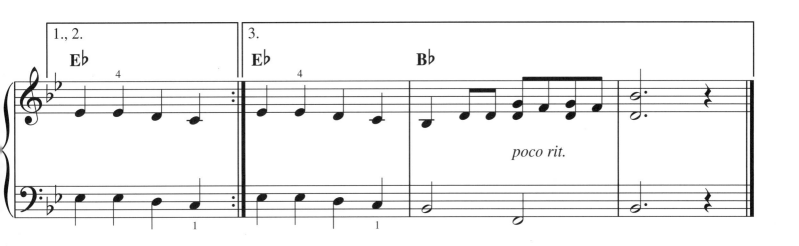

ORANGE BLOSSOM SPECIAL

Words and Music by
ERVIN T. ROUSE

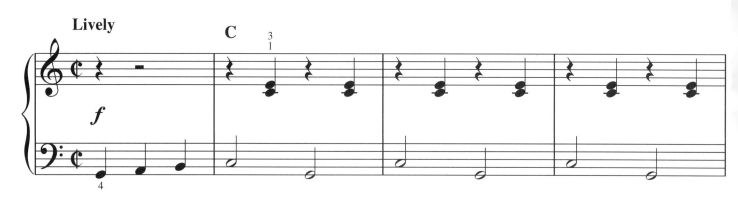

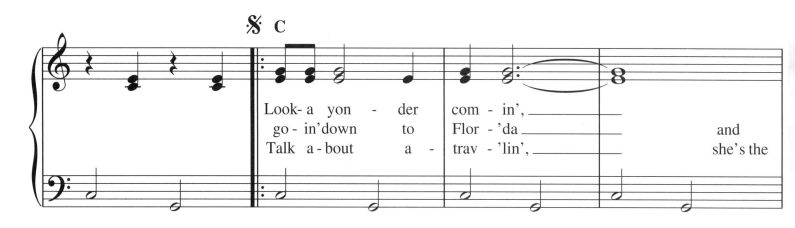

Look-a yon - der com - in', _____ and
go - in' down to Flor - 'da _____
Talk a - bout a - trav - 'lin', _____ she's the

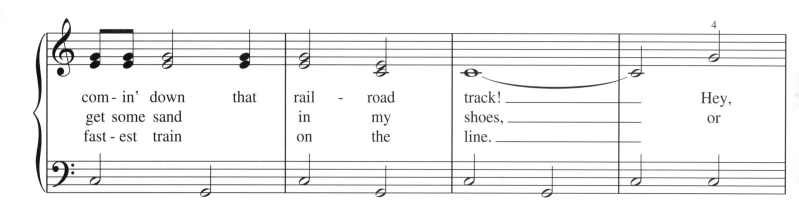

com - in' down that rail - road track! _____ Hey,
get some sand in my shoes, _____ or
fast - est train on the line. _____

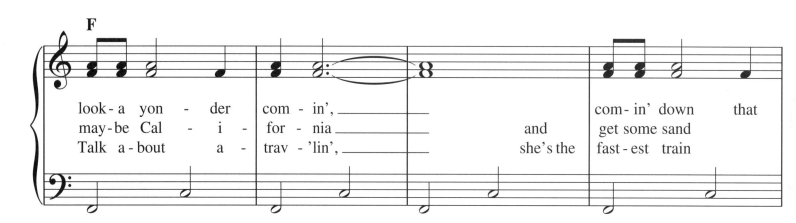

look-a yon - der com - in', _____ com - in' down that
may-be Cal - i - for - nia _____ and get some sand
Talk a - bout a - trav - 'lin', _____ she's the fast - est train

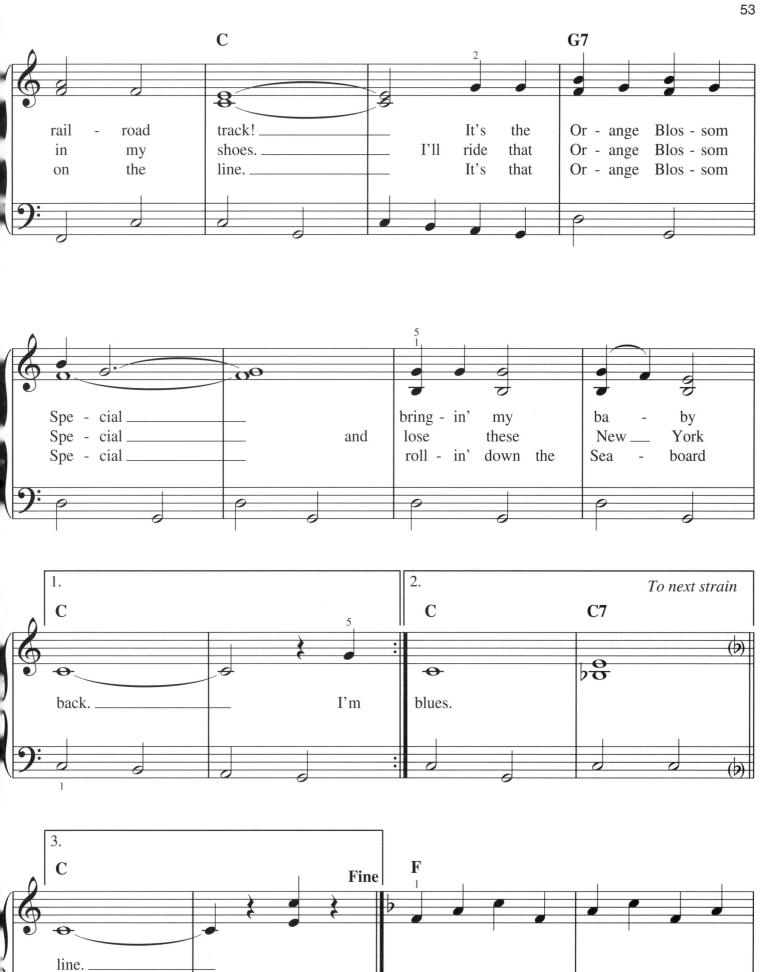

54

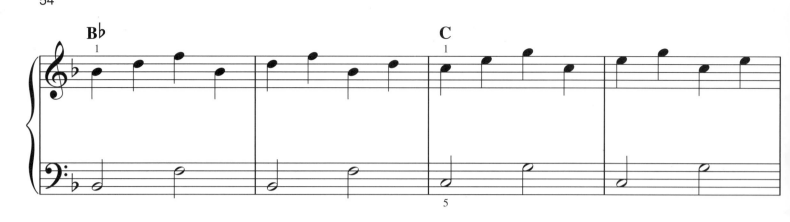

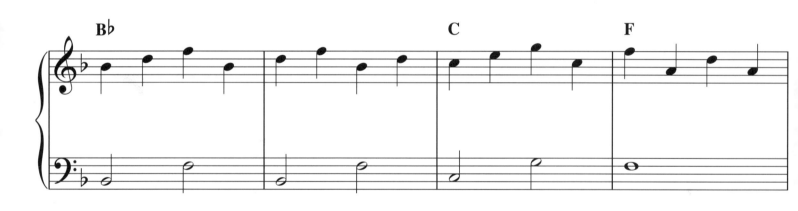

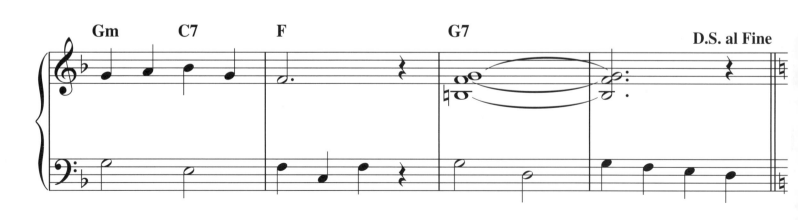